A H W I N D

Uncollected Poems, Young and Old

Carolyn Stoloff

MadHat Press
Asheville, North Carolina

MadHat Press
MadHat Incorporated
PO Box 8364, Asheville, NC 28814

The Library of Congress has assigned
this edition a Control Number of
2014915659

ISBN 978-1-941196-08-3 (paperback)

Text by Carolyn Stoloff
Cover photograph by Marc Vincenz
Book and cover design by MadHat Press

www.MadHat-Press.com

PREVIOUS BOOKS

Stepping Out – Unicorn Press
Stepping Out – New Rivers Press (chapbook)
Dying to Survive – Doubleday and Company
Lighter-Than-Night Verse – Red Hill Press (chapbook)
Swiftly Now – Ohio University Press
A Spool of Blue, New and Selected Poems – Poets Now series,
     Scarecrow Press
You Came to Meet Someone Else – Asylum Arts Press
Greatest Hits – Pudding House Press (chapbook)
Reaching for Honey – Red Hen Press

PRAISE FOR PREVIOUS COLLECTIONS

"Through Carolyn Stoloff's painter's eyes, a bright swarm of images rushes by us and we are filled with a sense that the world is luminous, spiritiually alive, and ready to speak to us."

—John Balaban

Of *Dying to Survive*: "Carolyn Stoloff reveals herself as a stoic traveler, spiritually and geographically. There is a modern, emancipated woman's sensibility throughout her work; loneliness is the unspoken, profound assumption—but never self-pity...."

—*Publisher's Weekly*

Of *Swiftly Now*: "The poems in *Swiftly Now* begin crisp and vivid. The sequence gathers power as one reads, and the final climactic poems are stunning in their clarity and penetration."

—May Swenson

Of *A Spool of Blue*: "There is an excitement, a liveliness, in the world of Stoloff's poetry...There is verve in her poetry reminiscent of the verve in good O'Hara poems and those jazzy paintings of Piet Mondrian, such as 'Broadway Boogie-Woogie'."

—*Library Journal*

AH WIND

Uncollected Poems, Young and Old

CONTENTS

I

II

IV

I

AGAINST THE SHINING WIND
Brooklyn Botanic Garden

idling beneath trees, I close my palm
against shining wind
that would take

the print of grass from my cheek

spring's sometime will never come,
I think, skin deep in shells
in calcium petals

in the white tree top,
waist deep, a girl in red

her hands' open doors
frame darkness, her mouth
calls down the corridor

between cherries blossoming

she calls her horse
still far away   calling,
she feels a thundering not hoofs

her blood gallops

I had forgotten how wind
knocks blossoms down

THE MAN WITH GREY EYES
for F.H.

boats balance on swells and ripples
his hair feels soft as ashes,
water and ashes in the wind

his eyes—halfway up the sky
on a clear day—look down
on small dead birds,

on islands without fresh water,
on bizarre freight in holds of boats
in the harbor, boats

in passage and along wharfs
his eyes—a highway for birds
with grey breasts and crests....

boats balance in swells and ripples
hard and narrow as a mast,
as a flagpole, his body bends,

climbs reaches his body—
a bridge hanging from the sky—
feels a boat pass under it,

a freighter with furniture
in her hold, again and again

AROUND ONCE AGAIN
for F.H.

I'll lean against you
you, against the cabin
no need for bridges
Manhattan flows by
you identify smoke stacks
your camera eye catches
a flock of red cranes
rusted springs
an anchor on the dock
my face sticky
with clam juice

airy as warm bread
we'd feel the trumpets
and solemn drums
watch the Madonna lurch
on her palanquin
above sweating men

around once again
before the bread cools
and boys in leather
slump in doorways
before the fish man dies

leaving his fresh trout
in the freezer
leaving my mind
still as a white river

I HAD JUST PAUSED

to gaze from my studio window
at water tanks under coolie hats
wearing thin belts around bellies
hoarding our treasure,

when spring's conductor, busy
punching air with green exclamations,
caught me dreaming,
tugged me out the door to stations
where my gaze rose above

dachshunds and tai chi,
through pink and white blooming parasols,
past the Chinese-lantern-like nest
wasps left in a cherry tree

the old springs return—warm waves
I lean into, naturally, the way I knew
dawn would break in a certain man's eyes—
clear, electric—and it did

what buzzing high-watt afternoons
we shared, what charged evenings—
a luminous union....
until the brownout

while, back at my studio, Selavy
one knee crossed on the other,
clutched his pipe and considered
adding a dot of cadmium red
to a night forest

TOWARD THE BLIND LIGHT

I too hear the gulls squeal
but it's you who rise,

lift your shirt from a neat pile
on the wooden chair
and button up

halfway, you pause
slide me a rich
closed smile

I become a long vowel
you occupy
the jacket you slip into
like a sword its sheath

pale with dawn
your full-moon cheek
touches mine

I move too
a road of light on water
where small swells
spread like a madness

without freight
on quiet soles, you travel
across my floor

HOW IT WAS

I'd pull the curtain aside   and Behold!
Venus—particle in my eye

or, if I felt bold, Eros
staining the whole world rose

silence with wings took my breath,
a glance sped circles of possibility
through the pond

there was the time, walking alone
in a scrimmage of green,
my raincoat a tent against deer flies,
sound enveloped me—unworldly harmonies

I bared my head—no wind,
no brass, no violins
was I the instrument?

> now the litter-tree sheds
> reams of published histories
> handwritten dream notes
> scraps from journeys that bloomed
>
> the postman delivers a bundle
> fresh bills gust in
> I'm raking and raking

there was a time on Capri....
alongside a donkey, his ears thrust
through holes in a straw hat,
cart filled with budding branches,

I'd climb the hill to gaze without purpose
over the locked vault of the sea

there was an uncluttered time
I'd slip into Vermeer's room
where the wall map is dim,

where milk's perpetual flow begins
at the crock's lip, where a pearl
glows on the scale pan

THE BALANCE

a palinode

it's called A Woman Weighing Pearls
but there's nothing on either tray!

only one white dot on the lip of each

come to think of it, why weigh pearls
what counts is the luster

might as well weigh light,

igniting fur on the plackets
and cuffs of the woman's blue jacket

light, from a high small window

falling across the curve of her brow
and on her fingers holding a chain
fastened to a bar

from it scale pans depend
in front of her swelling abdomen

behind her on the wall, a painting—

dim figures gesture
below a hovering Christ in his aureole,

come to judge souls

the light in the studio also rests
on her hand, firm on the table
to achieve steadiness,

permitting the balance to level

how would this scene weigh in?

first the canvas, fine linen no doubt,
then the pigment-dust ground in oil,

brushed on by Vermeer,
picking out forms and textures
highlighted by sun

leaving the flat Resurrection in gloom

our eyes see depth

we peer into the room—a hushed
corner, preserved
by the grace of light

from beyond that Delft street

JEALOUSY

the child squirms against papa's knee
insisting with work-song intensity
that he **come** to lift her so she can swing
from the high pole, that he **come** away
from the beaming woman with the lemony
smell who minced over the skyline
in her crocheted hat and now sits
close to him stroking his cheek with her eyes
that he ***come on***

resting along the bench back,
papa's arm must be glued to the woman
the warm child-hand takes his square one
and tugs ***come on, come on***
can you touch your nose with your tongue?
can you?   she shows him how....
skips back, pulling him,
his hand sandwiched in hers now

he lifts her high with a laugh
and gives a shove *wheeeee*
she swings from nine to three
her dress flares like a sea anemone
she spreads her legs as she rides high
buds redden on the bare trees

ON THE SUBWAY PLATFORM

the boy holds his mother's hand
his father talks intensely in a foreign tongue
using arm and hand for emphases
the boy tilts his face up
and reaches for the arm

he captures it
pulls the man's hand toward the woman's hand
putting his face against the two
the father breaks loose
and goes on talking

the child smiles exposing little white teeth
his gaze follows the hairy arm
as though it were a small monkey   as though he
were a young dog watching a bee
his hand goes after it

wishing to join mother to father he gently
draws attention down to the living
bond between them
the mother listens to the man
heeding the boy through an ear in her belly

now pressing the child's cheek to her side
she looks down briefly   then
over the boy's head she answers the man
speaking intensely

SEA'S EDGE

a small boy runs to his mother on the sand
the rock died the boy says

mother follows his finger, her eyes
sliding over high tide's smooth coverlet,

laughing at the thought
of a living rock

but the boy knows....
he has played with it

he splashes into the surf again
and waves from his perch on the hidden hump

he calls to his mother and waves
but his mother has leaned back

in her lounge chair, lids closed
to the sun's glare, screening the image of a man

on the platform of a station passed
this morning, a man framed

in a train window
then wiped away

Carolyn Stoloff

SHOULDERING THE SHOULDS

when fathers left
with instructions held high on sticks
we swung till we could swing no higher

rid of their top hats and canes
trampling new-mown grass
we circled the school with a stranger's dog
taking turns with the leash

Jim tried on an abandoned shirt
Artie helped me chase trash
escaped from the bin

I hollered you don't tie up big dogs *like that*

a boy climbed from the ditch
watching the girl who had chased him
now absorbed in her own body
as she folded over the pole and flopped

watch out I called as Anne swung too high
and the chain slackened
but she had already dragged her feet in the dirt
and run off to the highest slide,

where she hung from the top rail
the one you hold on to—
legs set in front—until you let go

you know you're not 'sposed to
I panted running toward her

but she was down and around the corner
leaving me breathless

Carolyn Stoloff

TIME, DROP BY DROP, AND THE TIDE

in the crowd at a bus stop, each soul
holds its drop apart

the flow catches us—boys who slide,
yelping, toward lily skirts, giggling girls
who twirl out of reach

the tide has no patience with divisions
or visions : the librarian's wish to plunge
into the young farmer's chest,

the child crouched under the table
who thinks he's invisible

mourning, a feature of tides, runs
below laughter on a home-bound bus
when old girls prolong an outing,

masking the buzzing in each brain
with noisy commotion

couples who kiss kiss kiss may guess
the conveyor belt end
in a resort without rooms,

a space where no 'other' is

but the saint who feels a deep
moist melancholy in his folds
lets the blissful flood take him

MOURNING CELEBRATION
for Ann McMillan, composer

whose arachnid fingers no longer spin sound-webs
    for the sensuous hours
no longer wrap insect minutes in string concerti
no longer capture the buzz among dahlias
to release in her auditory garden

always close to earth, the composer
    crouched among marsh reeds to listen
she taped fiddling crickets and a thrush song
    in the forest
to dissect and reassemble

for those drawn to her room, a box filled
    with weavings, bones and seed pods,
she'd beat the cosmic egg to cook for us
    with nasturtiums or pimientos

the composer's ebullience flames amid bursting
    pinecones....
reduced now to ashes in an urn too full
    to resonate
no matter whose gypsy hands tap its broad hips
no matter how soft the lips
whispering Ann Ann to the obsidian stopper

now that she's gone who will feed her cat?
who will bottle those firefly delights!
who will blast sorrow's boulder so its crumbs
    can be washed and strained for garnets?

in the navy blue hours, I remember Ann's calls
    now too high for the human ear
at dawn I've found gossamer—her fine white
    hair—
here and there in a meadow

NOT BY APPOINTMENT

I see a tall slim man capped by silver hair—
    through steam from a manhole,
    in an A & P
        bending to retie his sneaker,
    in the dim lobby of a Paris hotel—

and my breath quickens

I sense you behind me
    as I search the sky over Central Park
    for the heron
or when I peer through a botanist's lens
    at a fuzzy stem

you're gone when I turn

on the street I hear your name called
    by people to whom you mean nothing
your name means forthright,
    honest in speech
I recall your eyes, hands, waist,
    separately

Scorpio's your sign

last night, from sleep's immensity,
    you were reborn,
without sting, smiling,
shaped with dream-filings stored by day
    in a jar on a shelf
    too high to reach

between us one heart

submerged in dark radiance, I nestled
    against you....
in deep

THIS SPRING

last year's shrivelled apple shifts
in wind that snatches pollen
from cradling white and pink so
soon unsnapped rocked loose so soon
oh see the blossoms

slalom down air's slopes numinous
as motes in sun numberless as notes
exchanged by novices who learning love
rehearse its rounds and canons disguised
as common calls but untranslatable
as intervals a lark shapes

old/new messages slide under eyelids fall
into chutes glide behind mail flaps down
ear corridors past aliases walls biases
one way to the heart's altar round trip
to seasons' revolving core in the Earth-drupe

what can be built with this freshness?
enough that spring comes to pass with scents
that linger around nerve-tree stations
dallying among these pollen nurses who
when a gust dismisses them
leave purses filled with being's hum

II

WHERE ROADS CROSS
Vence, France

turn left for town and market, right
for the mineral spring—just short
of the freshly painted Christ
nailed to his tree

it's evening   at her high window,

the old moon peers
down mountain roads to see
who steals toward rendezvous
in shadows cypress hedges throw

but love won't stop her waning

before the owl swoops for its prey
fill a bottle at the source so night
begets dawn—a child who holds up
shining minnows in a pail

his pride needs no translation

if water infinitely springs
it's drawn downward without mercy
at each step roads uncross
no one can die for us

PLAZA DE DOÑA ELVIRA
Seville, Spain

I

wooden door
red roses in a basket
now O whistling boy
pass beneath the shade
of correct orange trees
to the fountain

on tip-toe
in open sun, stretch
to catch the hard spray
on your palate
as I catch your spirit
in my mouth,

its taste of green
and bitter orange

II

two women wing fans
against noon
snap them shut
cross the plaza toward rooms
darkened against beams
of passionate sun

two women stride
between clapping men
whose eyes
collect women
who expose them to the skin
with words that tumble
like spilled shot

two fans hum
as firm women wing
through honey noon
to dapple dark—
a patio's cool corolla

Carolyn Stoloff

III

a false moon snaps on
in an orange tree
a young man holds the true moon
under his tongue as he sings
to the hollow woman-wood
in the curve of his chest
sings through its barred window
into shadow

on a bench three young girls
discreetly squirm
three trim girls turn
gypsy as mosquitoes drone
and the fountain climbs the light
of a lamp's false moon

from a window a woman calls
to the three girls who rise
glance sidewise at the man
serenading his guitar
as they walk to the wooden door
each with his mellow
voice in her veins   each full
each aching

ANIMAL, VEGETABLE, MINERAL
Nerja, Spain

on certain days
the eye at my keyhole glows—
large as a melon

the gate's come ajar

my neighbor's black goat
crops weeds in my yard
his dusty brow presses my thigh

from a field nearby
the ploughman's long call yokes
him through his ox to mineral

seated, palm to chin, I feel
a lizard glide over my toes
a fly on my knee begins washing its wings

a voice blows in—
the woman's scolding her son

ordained by common breath, I pardon him

at noon nothing sharp threatens
above me—in the frugal blue—
a yellow melon cradles
seeds of my burial

Carolyn Stoloff

SPAIN

ivy   its irrepressible need to climb
                              torn from my limbs

above this hill   in air drunk with dusk
cloud tendrils ignite

                head low a white ox plods the road
a man's long call urges him on

                a moment can't be opened   but
                              within the chapel's walls
centuries transpire

across a hay-strewn floor   light from candles
flickering on the gilt *retablo* beckons
                as though it were the goal

stay?   if I feasted with priests
roast ox would taste sweet
                              as sweet as betrayal

go?
an empty horizon awaits my inventions
                              with ravenous appetite

BETWEEN POINTS

Spain

black goats balance on the mountain
as darkness begins
we call across vast distance

old women in black
weave behind wind

outside the gate, another gate
burdened with bags, we wait

I've seen a flayed sheep's teeth
gleam like Christ's
through a skin of blood

Carolyn Stoloff

IN THE NEW HAMPSHIRE WOODS

the woodpile shrinks
hour by hour

the chipmunk who lives there
nervously scratches his side

a fire must be fed continually

the sun escapes
we drag him home to the hearth

it rained last night

jays scrape the glass air
with rusty shrieks

I walk
under the candelabra-pines
making promises to myself

on each needle tip, a drop—

a sparkle
the afternoon sun extinguishes

HOLIDAY

we roll to our backs
arms flung wide
and smile at the sky
where wind plays with hay

the camera dozes on three legs
wounds in carved stone
close again we are young
gods today

may it always be this way

let men shoot in the woods
let cats circle a distant robin
let mice record dim shapes
in the temple

here, on the mown field
light sings—a rare pitch

how sweet the roast thigh smells!
we roll to our sides, laughing

Carolyn Stoloff

CASUALLY

he took me on casually—
chuckling, he hooked in
to my privacy

I broke out laughing

we circled
chatting mulberries

he mentioned a lost lighter
marriage, a motel
and love

he spoke casually

we crouched
buttons struggled
against buttonholes

something bright
moved in the leaves

I threw him a plum
told how the wings
fell from my scapulae

we dropped
through each other's eyes
once, not casually

a grosbeak
exposing its red stain
sang

white whiskers bloom
on the plum pit
in my ashtray

he's turned
grave now
peeling years, I grieve

on the blade

THE GIFT

I said *yes* to day's
raucous blue, rabbit clouds
scudding above the deserted mill

then an actual fox...poised
on a boulder by the dam

I faced him seconds
real as a dog
the color of rust and granite

watched him race
across the greensward into trees
packed to make a mystery
carrying his comfort in his ribs

at the edge
where leaves squalled down, I bent
to gather acorns

we'd stood eye to eye
for seconds

come back!
why were you not hiding?
look how the sky's

breaking into jays
let us...together (why not?)
....into the woods

I go on, cross lines
where beavers drag young poplars
from the hill,

toss acorns to the pigs
greedy always

Carolyn Stoloff

TURNING POINTS
Peterborough, N,H.

plop a closed lily drops

water gleams in a jar

and beyond the half open door
dust, heaped up

a breeze
dismisses leftover gestures

the wasp escapes

never mind
someone will come

leaves tap the window

sky draws
to its breathless close

against a lamp-lit room
the hour flutters
pressing its pale belly to glass

sometimes across night
a familiar arm....

the hand bows
an old tune on a violin

clouds part

exposing a whole note
one could drown in

Carolyn Stoloff

NEAR ROUTE 101

trucks rumble on route 101
stuffed with rubber breasts

and ropes to hobble
where is the calf? the bull?

in her cold cellar, mother
shrinks to her roots

I reach down the hole
touching my father's shoulder

rivals listen intently
dropping dung in the field

in rooms thick with guests
the past crowds in and the gnats

but someday, on a main artery,
I'll greet Death—

lifting my skull-pan
like a hat

IN THE RUIN
Peterborough, N,H.

an emptied glass
fox eyes on the road
night is near, in back—
a speeding car

where the floor was swept
a pile of leaves
a hand shines a window
with no frame

a dog barks

the sun's wedged
between oaks

on a fallen beam.
an ear, a snail....

there's a sound
of scurrying feet
where the roof used to be

be quiet ferns
stop uncurling
soon night will foreclose
everything

Carolyn Stoloff

DAWN IMPROMPTU
Ossabaw Island, Georgia

a grunt heaves up
from under a palmetto

sky, pink as a shell's lining,
tints the bay

there go the ducks...cutouts
in a line   afloat
on the stillness

a milk-glass moon hangs low

but day, crackling,
chases night
into my crushed napkin

a live-oak grove
beyond this patio sends out
an urgent *ratatatat*

far away a donkey brays

vampire fairies
move in to strip-mine my veins

I slap myself slapping them

a butterfly falls settles
tastes my scrawl with soles
thin as hairs

if that devil-pig charges
I'll toss him a camellia

pigs were the first tillers

ADOBE HOUSE

for Lawrence Calcagno, painter
in memory now Taos, N.M.

the man circled his apricot tree
walked the garden wall
up a pole to the roof

he watered every shrub   green fruit
fell with leaves and limbs
as he groomed the atrium

this is *my* house
I own this house, he said
laying a hand on her flank

she opened her hub
her hundred-and-one year chambers
letting him get familiar

My interior, he whispered
touching each inside
corner with eye or finger

then, moving his candle though her,
he cast his shadow
on the walls, on the wide floorboards,

in the earth well
that owned him

TOWARD THE HORIZON'S SILL
Taos, N.M.

my toes touch a rough doormat
stretching west to the sill

the hegira lengths
of ant generations

toward distant pyramids
evening descends

§

in my palm
a warm bird nests

high up, cottony fish
discharge glazed eggs

a few large drops
cling to limbs like stars

§

a staircase, the citrus light
descends now

and willow leaves—
loose hair of old Indians

Carolyn Stoloff

I braid my time
the clouds' flowing manes

§

dark horses lift their heads

AT THE FOOT OF THE HOLY
Taos, N.M.

twig web cast on a wall
quivers

pungent ooze from wounds
where bark split....

taffeta transitions spill
through ear corridors

and laughter of children
swiftly cycling

wild rose leaves vibrate
on the bush—

Dubonnet, carmine—
a paisley shawl to wrap
my eyes in

behind me bees bumble
among late mums

and the mountain opens
a fist of silver pebbles

if I don't run, I'm moved

Carolyn Stoloff

with sun-soaked wafers
spinning downwind

to thicken
at the shadow's foot

As Evening Erases Day's Entries
Taos, N.M.

to the west molten gold lingers
on the hills' undulating lip

shade, issuing from burrows
and cracks in pine bark, gathers
to fill the valley's bowl

remote lark notes
from a high-meadow fence-post
depend on stillness

brushed by dusk's cool breeze,
someone breathes

Carolyn Stoloff

ARIZONA HIGHWAY

the traveller stops, perplexed
an ambivalent white line divides the lanes
but no one's on the road

lamps click on
light shrinks to a lime streak in the west
she strides to a timetable on a shop window

sensing a presence she shifts her focus
to a shadow settling across cards
with wishes for good voyages

she could turn...inquire about departures
but no   what if the last bus
left with its load—dozing passengers,

hands overlapped, self coupled with self,
wheeling one way or the other
into the dark

at her back a whisper....
sand shifting?
a eucalyptus shedding its bark?

III

SOUNDING

held upright in a glass
even water
    casts a shadow

an ink-spill despair
       clings to my soles
it stretches and shrinks

I search for its face
    until my eyes tear

at dusk when shadows pool
I sink
    to a fixed location
beside a piano stool

mother points
    to where I come in
father plucks his mandolin

blackbirds on the staff
    take wing
the wind speaks Russian

our trio soars as I sing
about a white birch
    and a pack I carry

by the sun-boulder
   in a blue meadow
I shake off my shoes
   my shriveled shadow

into a clear reservoir
   song pours me

How We Took to the Road

when the burning ball
dropped
in its hole

and the mountain closed
over it,

we jumped on a hayrack
smoking blackness
death's tobacco

reins smacked a rump
we fell back, laughing,
sneezing in straw

yellow stars up our sleeves
we sang
to the wind's harmonica

we knew
jackal men weighing stones
lurked
between home and home

muffling our terror
we groped
under night's cape

Carolyn Stoloff

for the mountain-horn

for a cave
with its spark, dead center

To Jerusalem

at night
on the room's field
old games trap us—

grave circles, lines
worn now
overlapping

thick numbered figures,
leaping
against barricades,

reach
into the net
for a moon

and the clock....
what can be said of it?
keeping, passing

one goal post to the next
chair to chair
hands, bearing

a basket of blood
to Jerusalem

MAD IN A GLASS BOOTH

mad in a glass booth
losing blood
changes swallowed
by the clanging box
heart-beast
fold your webs—too weak
no tool to break banks
or talk with

clumsy bundle
permanently
disconnected
day drowns your beat
fold your webs
what ought to be is not

who wants your pelt!
your pockets your pressure
deep and close
your rodent unborn love
your inner face
sealed in its black jar
like a sunrise

SOMETHING UNEASY

lying against earth, and you,
something uneasy hungered
it was not enough to dream, to follow
figures camouflaged in clouds

we caught the ant hour
frantic on a blade, the last fish,
limp and milky in the creel
and wanted more:

to watch the self die,
to love with forceps, peeling bark aside
sealed in galls our yearnings
swarmed, luscious in aberration

here, where two cold women on a porch
backed to greenly gleaming windows
rock and judge across the lawn,
catch talk and then repeat it,

I long for that dis-ease, that hunger

WE DANCE

steel shot covers Earth   when women
can't laugh they dance

children have stopped playing to watch,
dangling plump legs

from hard chairs they watch
clutching long-eared balloons,

watch us lean as though feet
were flowers, watch motion spill

men watch women rise from water,
watch them bend between children

blood river not mine, I have lost you
we are all brave, we who dance

A QUESTION OF BLUE

under luminous balloons
where panthers doze,

I swallowed the child-king
bewitched
by his question

he holds tight
to my heart,

tastes my salt
before the pacing fox

beneath my white uniform
he swells
in his question

his crown
rises in my throat

when my foot leaves earth
I'll bear him beyond
this ape house
and anxious birds

into that immense blue
I cannot explain

Carolyn Stoloff

TULIP POWER

the sight of a yellow tulip
peels me down to the child
who sees fish shapes in buttonholes,
daydreams pagodas, nets pollywogs,
hides in a glee of terror

yellow tulips in a row
revive quick eyes that catch
a thistle's ghost-star leaving home,
watch it rise, won't let go
till it's lost in sky

tulips renew a gaze
charmed by protean cloud-shadows
gliding across hills,
by flashing motes in a sun-stream,
by a caterpillar's billows

a tulip's blazing gaiety
brings back racing feet, feet
that scramble up day's rungs
then kick the ladder away
to fly in sleep over cities

faced with that primal yellow, I
am child-possessed entirely

GYRO

the change arrives—coins,
then his palms encompass
her upturned hand   charged
by this small tenderness

she walks away, a smile
smoothing nicks around her lips,
her heel-taps bright
on the deserted street

at the crossing, signals click
though there's no traffic—
like lights on a Christmas tree
when everyone's asleep

the taste of spicy meat
still in her mouth, she feels
the heat of his Greek
eyes on her back her   hips

sway in the old way
as a hanger on its pole
will swing, briefly
when freed of a winter weight

Carolyn Stoloff

PICKING UP STITCHES

bland as a trade wind
he spoke of his children
and summer vacations

one hand held a pipe
the other drooped
over his thigh

when a palm—warm
Mediterranean—
slipped from a sleeve

to touch my breast
cupping it
like a melon

suddenly seams came
together—not our pattern,
certainly not simple

and the needle
stitched up a gale
as though the machine

had gone crazy

BAD TIME

sharing litanies about failing mothers
we parted candlelight from dusk
then a hush fell

listen, I said, even a crippled journey
fulfills passage   a day
unfolds like a washed shirt, still stained

I grasp it, I lose it, I wear it

running to keep up with what won't let go
each of a us mourned a friend
both listened,

as if listening could guarantee
the trout's return to his pond

no, it's down the hill with an empty pail
gathering a few berries
a *hi* in passing

the immediate unfolds
like a shirt or sail
overnight mists lift   this morning

I touch joints of a net—ports

LAST NIGHT NEWS OF AN UNCLE'S DEATH REACHED ME
Sweetbriar, Virginia

long ago his voice rode sweet pipe smoke
bright teeth gleamed below
a full auburn mustache
now strangers stuff his pipes
scrape ash from the blackened cups

I hear a mooing through mist—
the morning freight headed west

who's picking crumbs from his overcoat pocket?
who's brushing dust
from underneath its fur collar?   he'd a taste
for wine, fine tweeds, escargots
a gold chain looped from his vest

here, grass springs back after cows pass
here two hounds sniff for scraps
near an old picnic table—a bier,
it invites uncle, onyx uncle,
drained of taste and appetite

near the end did aunt wipe your chin?
did she comb your thin hair,
stroke your pale freckled hand?

in your lungs grand operas expired
your honeyed tongue sleeps, stiff, in its cradle
there's a package, unclaimed, in my uncle-depot,
a small bundle, our several exchanges

sliding over my scalp once, your fingertips
groped for mounds of distinction
once aunt sent me with you
to your bench by the river   a red carnation
bloomed in your buttonhole

at this hour, aunt's hooking her back brace,
wrapping her dragon-kimono around it
here, his neice awaits uncle's absence

here, a red bird streaks over the meadow

VISIT HOME

mamma keep keys in a pickle jar
each key has a white label
but she can't recall which door
they fit, or where the locks are
she will look for the canister
with the lock in it—tomorrow, if
she feels well enough

mamma's distressed
she flutters from room to room
in a housedress with frilly lace
at the collar trying to soothe....
trying to make things smooth
and nice for poppa

who is not well
who upsets his cereal bowl
and tears the napkin from his collar
who jumps up from table
shouting and scowling
mamma tries so hard....
it tires her

harsh noises are not good for her
but she feels bad for poppa
who is not well   she carefully prepares
his warm milk, dry toast and cereal
with his patients he was very jovial,
very skillful...the perfect host,
she reminds me

poppa can't see
too well now   when he bends over
in the hall, he can't see
to put the key in   he lifts
his glasses and wipes his good eye
the bunch of keys jangle

it came to mind last night how handsome
I thought poppa was when I lived home
and how he is not handsome
and how he is getting on
last night I took the keys
and opened his apartment door for him

Carolyn Stoloff

AFTERNOON BY THE SAILING POND

we're side by side on a bench
all afternoon   "soothing"
my mother says softly, her chin
gives a quick lift to where
oval lights like goldfish swim
in the blue a tree casts on grass

her gaze follows my finger
to a white muffin cloud poised
above a concrete and glass
high-rise dotting its **i**
then slips back to a sailboat's
broken reflection

a girl skates past us
a man launches a sloop
and leans on his pole
absorbed in his ship's white wing
with one thrust the mast aspires
and penetrates, reflecting

I'd like to be that way—
in passage, crossing my mother's
transparent stillness
leaving no scar

WHAT HAPPENED

                    to the memoirist who sent me the
                    excerpt about our first meeting

what's one dry leaf in November's gusts!
one day from a life   yet

each of us peers through a lens
at decades of foliage, hunting that day

our facts don't correspond   we do

I've read the pages you sent....
dug up carbons of letters to friends

your notes can't say what you quote—
clichés we never use

if that leaf were caught—evidence
projected with back light,

without sap
without its dance in wind,

find me the jury who'd sit through
the *I said...he/she saids*

hand tightening around my pen, I think:

each of us has good reason : a hat
with a flexible wide brim

to pull down on any aid against sun

and dour lines—yours, mine—
lifelines, entwined long since

VOYAGE OF THE SELF THAT DREAMS

springs creak as the dreaming self escapes
its skin to glide up the road, any road:
water, air...past tense Dobermans.
past Listerine lights, to board the dream

the ship lifts off with its strangers
exchanging crowns and masks or,
noses to portholes, searching for bright isles,
abandoned ballrooms in the vastness

and always the needs needs more——power,
profits, praise...more shining, before
we're drawn back by waking limbs
to choreographies of chores

then the last descent to a sealed bed
in a dank room where turnips root,
to hear through boards the music
of Cerberus snarling

IV

BE TAKEN AT DUSK

when you've culled every rose
            in the cumulus garden
and sun's burning parachute sinks

spin a line

drift, light as a newborn spider,
to where dune grass whisks
            graffiti in sand

step into the waiting craft
and push off
            feathering your oars
as notes slip back to music—
            slaps on the hull
            gulls' cries
            creaking locks

play with sky's hem
bouncing among liquid hills

be taken under
            with rusted engines
            torn sails

to the bed of sound

as bell-buoys ring
the sleeping tongue
    steers from within

what wants to save itself sings

INHERITANCE

those who sleep out of doors
have something not mine
for them home is everywhere

birds know their own chords
songs sown into them
apples drop clutching their cores

my heart depends on a vine
speech is its fruit—
something mine and not mine

Carolyn Stoloff

To My Hat

hat, my hutch,
protect me from flies

who plunge probosces
into tender inventions—

inclinations toward blue
or variations on the letter *I*—

as though by legal authority

tilted, an old umbrella
against Sun—that father

who flays us to ward off night—

shield against laughter,
felt crown,

set me inches above others

hide the soft rabbit

SOMEWHAT USED

leather skin, mine
by right of use, I'm rushed
through a chill universe
wearing you : glove,
skin, hand of love

a token from my heart
ticks in the turnstile
entranced, we pour
through synaptic doors
to encounters underground

hang on glove!
grip the democratic strap
and don't let go
no matter who's beside you
we're joined, hand heart mind
too the human chin

until the terrible tentacle
with a pull
strips you from my will
and drops us, outside into
the irrevocable bin

THE BUILDING

the building fills a space
it occupied before the bricks—
even the workmen's hours
persist in webs

paint-flakes snow upward
like continents
returning
to positions on the map

shadows caught behind paint
bleed back into corridors
to dwindle
like burning paper

pipes complain of eternal
darkness in the walls
but night
is everywhere

its spirit thickens
as light's last motion
wipes the husk
from its occupant

WHITHER

without hunger, without envy
why start out

it would take a lifetime to scout
the lineage of a gesture,

of one underthought
hung on a line in the wind

the thread slides between thumb
and forefinger

it could lead
from abstinence, across continents,

through tangled lianas
to a bloody groin

why work to collect cowries
what need for a viaticum

birds on a cable take off
even as one counts:

one   one   one
no doubt there were divas among them

but a throat
can't catch its truant voice

Carolyn Stoloff

To Go Easy

from a hedge, bird like a fist
shoots into wind, a sign....

he weighs his left fist on the scale
of his right palm, watching
a sail fill, herring gulls rise,

listening to the dry *clack clack*
as surf drags pebbles from the shore
he begins to fall, walking now,

hearing wind's sail-speech,
instinctively Polynesian—
sighs like blown monkey fur,

watching sails glide, gulls soar,
too careful to unfold, too schooled,
he weighs he sways, cautious still

not the great fish whose act
and wish are one, not the obtuse
boat or its willful captain

walking, he begins to be moved
a looser way

How We Inform

in a child's hand, the pencil
draws slow loops

a mule plods on
duty by duty

without wounds
can a field be sown?

goals rule roads
rulers, the school

an inch castles infinity

ants—an echo of running soldiers
whose war?   why?

a white shadow
crosses the dream's frame

flexed in sleep, nestling heads
wake to bruises

wind's no one's fault
ah wind!

breathed into, some words fly
in formation

NOTHING SHORT OF A MIRACLE

there is a lonely bell
a map without ports
a white bedroom with no dimension

oh the distance....
then the horizon's belt

sky meets sea
in silk harbors, in the lungs,
in petals sadly curled

in love's raft—a wafer
dissolving on night's tongue

DOWN TO SKY'S SOLES

a cloud drops   in the puzzling fog
my own hand escapes
hungry I steal toward the question,
stretch out at the feet of grass

throat, tongue, teeth, how did you learn
to play—"grass" for instance   I hear,
as if for the first time, wind's hiss in it
what fine instruments we are!

grass come forward   it's not clear today
what witchery you wear—
lawn green, crisp hay, or blade
held taut between thumbs to squeal

a wheat bud cracks—a flower
so small it remembers my shyness
a foghorn reaches   another replies
the calls augment—a round—

three low notes, dependable as cows
dear sound companions you give me bread,
feed me without hands

Carolyn Stoloff

OUT SKETCHING IN LATE AUTUMN

I start not to know
what I'm looking at   why
look so long if I lose it—
those violet woods way off
or whatever's outside,

as it becomes less or I
less (more likely) or its
it-ness nothing but Being
that fades as eyes hang on to
a mere grass spear,
a scarlet me-leaf
left on a twig that disappears

to catch on paper first sight
of trees stacked on sky,
space-making grass, rock,
is to lose what becomes
and to keep what was not
other than hand-made, mind-spun,
this day in autumn

OPENING

opening a stream I find the wrist
of an old woman   lifting the wrist
I touch vines still running with sap

I follow the sap between canyon walls
to the night wind's chapel

crossing the threshold I see
in the tabernacle of dawn
Earth's bristling pod

and crack it with my thumbs

from it our lifelines flow
like scarves through a magician's ring
they dissolve to my touch

cold seeds drift in space so dense
I can't see my hand opening

I don't feel my soles
or know my own gravity

if you hear this, answer
there's no tree anywhere

Carolyn Stoloff

WHEN SILENCE OPENS

night strokes my skin
cool as fresh sheets

it calms me

shhhh   no noise
we'll locate a point

a sustained note

over this mountain
or the next

climb with me

into the mine
between day-past and dawn

in its jaws an ant

carries an ember
along the dark corridor

INS AND OUTS

between us the tug-of-war
and a leaning
toward whispers

beyond us, Bach's
measurable
cleansing stream

how hidden we feel, yet
palpable
in the shuffle

from the wings
shade's amnesty
glides in

light slips
from fingers

what can be saved

shards from a vast dance
drift this way

acrobats
swing close
on air's cool trapeze

Carolyn Stoloff

dear barking joys
must you leave
us your departures?

still, deep
in the maze of my eye
a cedar grows

such splendor!

WHAT WILL COME

what will come?   noon
sweat pouring along creases
sun's biblical weight

there will be no waterhole, no relief
until evening arrives like a daughter
carrying death on a plate—
a charred fish
shedding scales on the dry bed
where each of us raises a tent.

as if wind would not lift dunes
in its tide, raking skin with sand
swallowing axes and bottles
bells, brains, marrow

while we watch for the caravan
risen from water—a sea
where whales and bright dolphins sing

On Schedule

spreading from the horizon's seams
glazing sea
tender as mist breathed
across a mountain's familiar breasts,

drawn through thickets and over bogs
creeping across granite, loam, concrete
and sleeping bodies,

despite avarice and blame
and how we force each other to our knees
and live in states of brokenness,

a brightening comes....

then the pink yolk spills
over Earth's rim, flooding everything

WIND

who can gauge wind's finesse when it whisks away
    spores with unseen fingers

or measure its width when it threads cracks
    too fine for a roach

who can count its pulse where pleas and complaints
    sing, as in a taut cable

faced with passionate gales, granite stands firm
    ....by stages it's ground to sand

much can be said about cargo a sea breeze carries
    the scent of ripe female wind brings

a man walks about with his flame of affection
    for the space of a held breath

then love's blown from its wick

by the same wind that leads through light's gate
    to the field where our atoms danced

until the Word shaped us

ACKNOWLEDGEMENTS

The author thanks the editors of publications where the poems in this collection first appeared (sometimes in earlier versions). They are as follows:

Part I of "Plaza de Doña Elvira" in *The Age of Koestler* (anthology)
"Jealousy" in *Antenna*
"Out Sketching in Late Autumn" and "Toward the Horizon's
    Sill" in *Aphros*
"Gyro" in *Barnabe Mountain Review*
"Arizona Highway" in *Birmingham Review*
"How It Was" and "Wind" in the *Bitter Oleander*
"Casually" in *Blue Buildings*
"To Go Easy" in *The Bridge*
"Opening" in *Caliban*
"Visit Home" in *Caprice*
"Whither" in *Contact II*
"In the Ruin" in *Embers*
"Mourning Celebration" in *Exquisite Corpse*
"Be Taken at Dusk" in *Hubbub*
"The Gift," "What Will Come," and "Between Points" in *Images*

Carolyn Stoloff

"Near Route 101" and "To Jerusalem" in *Invisible City*
"We Dance" and "Toward the Blind Light" in *The Little Magazine*
"Not by Appointment" in *The Montserrat Review*
"Against the Shining Wind" (as "Against the Shining Bird") in
    the *Nation*
"Down to Sky's Soles," "Tulip Power," "Where Roads" "Cross"
    and "When Silence Opens" in *Neovictorian/Cochlea*
"Shouldering the Shoulds" in *New Letters*
"Adobe House" in *Northwest Review*
"As Evening Erases Day's Entries" and "I Had Just Paused" in
    Oasis
"What Happened" in *Off the Coast*
"Dawn Impromptu" and "Spain" in *One Trick Pony*
"Voyage of the Self that Dreams" in *Open Unison Stop*
"Something Uneasy" (as "Something Diseased") in *Outsider*
"Picking Up Stitches" and "Animal, Vegetable, and Mineral" in
    Paintbrush
"On the Subway Platform," "Sea's Edge," "Last Night" and "News
    of an Uncle's Death Reached Me" in *Pembroke Magazine*
"Afternoon by the Sailing Pond" in *Poet Lore*
"The Balance" in *Poetry East*
"Mad in a Glass Booth" in *Poetry Northwest*
"A Question of Blue" in *Poetry Review, Tampa*
"Holiday," "To My Hat," "In the New Hampshire Woods" and
    "Around Once Again" in *Poetry Now*
"Somewhat Used," "Bad Time," and "Ins and Outs" in *Poets On*
"Sounding" in *Porch*
"The Man with Grey Eyes" in *Prairie Schooner*
"Nothing Short of a Miracle" and "How We Inform" in *Pulpsmith*
"At the Foot of the Holy" in *Ship of Fools*
"Turning Points" in *The Smith*
"The Building" in *The Southern Poetry Review*

"How We Took to the Road" in *Thunder City Review*
"Inheritance" and "This Spring" in *Yankee*
"Time, Drop by Drop, and the Tide" in *Yefieff*

ABOUT THE AUTHOR

Carolyn Stoloff, New York poet and painter, is the author of
Reaching for Honey (Red Hen Press), *You Came to Meet Someone
Else* (Asylum Arts), *A Spool of Blue: New and Selected Poems*
(Scarecrow Press), *Dying to Survive* (Doubleday & Co.), *Swiftly
Now* (Ohio University Press) and *Stepping Out* (Unicorn Press),
as well as two chapbooks, *Lighter Than Night Verse* and *In The Red
Meadow*. Her poems have appeared in such magazines as the *New
Yorker*, the *Nation, Cincinnati Review, Hotel Amerika*, the *Bitter
Oleander*, and *Bomb*, and in many anthologies including *The
New Yorker Book of Poems, New Directions 53*, and *Rising Tides,
A Year in Poetry*. Ms. Stoloff was awarded a National Council on
the Arts Award for achievement, the Theodore Roethke Award
from Poetry Northwest, and numerous other awards. She has also
visited the MacDowell Colony, the UCROSS Foundation, the
Wurlitzer Foundation, and the Virginia Center for the Creative
Arts, among other colonies. She taught both poetry and studio
art at Manhattanville College for many years. She also taught in
public schools, a house of detention, and a Quaker-run halfway
house for drug addicts.